The Road to Lilac Hill

Other Books by Barbara Drake

Poetry

Driving One Hundred (Windfall Press, 2009)

What We Say to Strangers (Breitenbush Press, 1986)

Love at the Egyptian Theatre (Red Cedar Press, 1978)

Chapbooks

Small Favors (Traprock Press, 2003)

Space Before A (26 Books Press, 1996)

Bees in Wet Weather (Canoe Press, 1992)

Life in a Gothic Novel (White Ewe Press, 1981)

Who's Responsible? (Stone Press, 1978)

Field Poems (Stone Press, 1975)

Narcissa Notebook (Stone Press, 1973)

Creative Nonfiction

Morning Light: Wildflowers, Night Skies, and Other Ordinary Joys of Oregon Country Life (Oregon State University Press, 2014)

Peace at Heart: An Oregon Country Life (Oregon State University Press, 1998)

Textbook

Writing Poetry (1st edition: Harcourt Brace Jovanovich, 1983; 2nd edition: Cengage Learning, 1994)

The Road to Lilac Hill

Poems of Time, Place, and Memory

Barbara Drake

Windfall Press • Portland, Oregon

First edition. Published December 2018.

Windfall Press
PO Box 19751
Portland, OR 97280

www.windfalljournal.com

Book design by Cheryl McLean, ImPrint Services.
Cover: Detail from a photo by James Ward "Kansas" Robertson
    showing Trask Mountain and the Oregon Coast Range
    as seen from Lilac Hill, 1987.
Author photo by William Beckman.

Drake, Barbara, 1939–
The road to Lilac Hill : poems of time, place, and memory /
    Barbara Drake
ISBN: 978-0-9700302-7-6
Library of Congress Control Number: 2018946475

Dedicated with love to my mother,
Monica Catherine Lorson Robertson,
a black-haired, blue-eyed beauty from Kansas

Contents

There are three times: a present time about things past, a present time about things present, and a present time about things future. The future exists only as expectations, the past exists only as memory, but expectation and memory exist in the present.
—St. Augustine

There's no time like the present.
—Old saying

1

The Seventy-Five-Year-Old Woman
Has Seen Wonders in Her Life

One was a blimp that flew over Cannon Beach in 1943
where I sat in the sand playing with my bucket and shovel.
Overhead a man opened a surprising door in the box below the airship.
He leaned far out and waved and I waved back at him.

Another was the garbage dump with pigs,
maybe that same year. Father warned me to stay in the truck
or the pigs would eat me up like a Cracker Jack.
They were monstrous big, both black and pink.
They rooted around the truck as I watched them
and father dumped our garbage.

The third wonder I shall describe was horses
pulling seine nets on the Columbia near Clatskanie.
Father said they were fishing. Far out on the water
a boat tugged the other end of the net,
which was full of salmon. The horses were giants.
Their strong necks curved like swans' necks.

You rarely see such things anymore—
two-lane highways from one end of the country to the other,
ladies with seams on the backs of their stockings,
liver and onions on restaurant menus.

My First Butcher

Bob's Superette, Eugene, Oregon, 1961

Dressed in white like a surgeon
he instructed me in the art of meat.
He was patient and considerate
to my young housewife self—
showed me how to look for marbling,
described what to do with the cheap cuts,
which to curry and which to Swiss.

Only plain white butcher paper would do.
There were no disguising dyes,
no plastic wrap or Styrofoam trays.

He told me
lean was best for meatballs,
half pork, half beef.
With burgers on the hibachi
a little fat was good.
His round, clean-shaven face
was pink above the display case.
We were good together.

Milky Coffee

Usually I don't want sugar in my coffee
but today I pour in a spoonful
and there it is, memory in sweet coffee:
I am fifteen, riding in the back seat
of an old Plymouth driven by Art,
my friend Bonnie's father,
because it's late at night and she is too tired
to drive back from Portland to Coos Bay,
and I am too young to drive at all.
The night before, Art, a kind but broken man,
pulled himself together after we found him
at his favorite tavern in Portland.
I waited on the sidewalk
under a streetlight with moths circling
and Bonnie, twenty-one, went in to get him.
Now, shaky but clean, Art sits at the wheel.

Bonnie wants to start her own business
raising night crawlers in a dirt box
back of the auto court, out by the slough.
She says we will sell them to fishermen
and make easy money.
Yesterday we counted out
ten thousand night crawlers on a farm
up on Prune Hill, outside Camas.
Now, with a trailer on the back of the Plymouth
we're taking them home.
There's dense fog from Otis Junction south,
not just fog but midnight fog

where you can't see the curve of the road
until you're in it. On our left I glimpse
leaning from the rocky bank
salal, monkey flowers, stunted coastal pines,
but in this fog I can't see the ocean
far below on the right.
Now as we drive south I fall asleep.
That's what fifteen-year-olds do.
And we go through dark and fog until
we stop somewhere, maybe Depoe Bay,
at an all-night café
on the east side of the highway.
I don't drink coffee yet but tonight
I order a cup as Bonnie and Art do.
I fill my bitter cup with cream and sugar—
a lot of it, so it's sweet and milky—then sip.
I'd never known coffee was this good.

I hold it, hot, with both hands, and as I drink,
something is etched on my mind,
something sweet and milky, something
along with the feeling of being lost
in the fog of life, but exciting too.
Taste of milky coffee and the thought
Someday I will be someone
come all at once. Later the fog clears.
Deep as the ocean that wafts and purls offshore
as we drive south, expectation, sweet coffee,
sweet milky memory, like all the rest,
settles down in me.

Kansas (1914–1992)

My father smelled of metal,
of solder and wire,
of stop bath, cigarettes, whiskey,
leather, airplanes, and coffee.

My father was tall like a telephone pole
and could walk into the sky on climbing hooks.
His hair was curly as lamb's wool
and his smile was crooked like a farm boy's hat.

When he was hungry, he was hungry.
And after he ate he would smile and say,
Funny, I'm not hungry anymore.
After he ate he'd take a nap.

People said of him, *That man, Kansas,*
can nap just about anywhere.
It didn't matter where—
a couch or the hood of a car.

He'd lie on his back, hands folded,
snore lightly for five minutes,
and then he was wide awake,
ready for the next thing.

Grace

Grandmother,
just when I thought you had receded
to a black-and-white photo in the picture box,
I suddenly see you
in my cup of tea this morning.
I remember before you died—
I was four years old—in a gentle voice
you asked me not to rock your chair too hard.
The rocking hurt your back.
Now I know what the pain was
and you were soon gone.

But after all these years, here you are again
in my blue and white cup
as I remember your favorite meal,
a boiled egg and a cup of tea
with milk and sugar. Now I am so much
older than you when you died
and memory alone
is insufficient unless set down.

You raised a lamb once,
a bummer who lived in the yard
and was fed by a bottle.
You also raised two boys
who liked to shoot, ride,
toss back a snort now and then,
tell stories with strangers.
They too are gone.
You nursed for a living when widowed,
turned the farm over to my parents
who soon left it for the West.

Grandmother, I want you to know
as long as I live you will be
one of my beloved ghosts,
bringing the sweet scent of Kansas grass
to pleasure in a cup of tea.
I drink my tea without the sweet
milk and sugar, but still you are there
in the shimmering amber of the liquid,
in the leafy smell of tea, like hay,
like sodden maple leaves in fall,
like the harvest smell of the world.

Nina, Kansas

It was always rough
in winter going out with a cough,
the stuck door, then snow-laden boughs,
the melting road like a slough.
It felt like walking through dough,
sloughing off sleep and pushing through
drifts to the watering trough
to break ice, the hiccough
of the old mule, the mournful sough
of the winter wind, the chough
of a crow in the woods, never enough
time to sleep. You had to be tough
or you'd just give up, though
sometimes a breakthrough
would keep you going: a mended plough,
baby chicks, the yeasty smell of sourdough
rising on the hot stove. Although
life was hard, hope was sometimes enough.

The Typist

I made 87½ cents an hour typing
when I was a college student.
I was a great typist.
My boss was a woman
who used a Stenorette,
a recording machine with a foot pedal,
to dictate puny little messages
about things that needed doing.

After I typed a message perfectly,
she would read it over, change a word
or two, and ask me to type it again.
While I typed, she'd grab her cigarettes,
go down to the coffee shop,
and drink coffee with The Director.
I could tell she thought he was cute,
but he was married.

I had a kind of scorn for her,
that she couldn't type her own messages,
that she couldn't get it right the first time,
that she did so little
and I was paid so little.

Posterity

For JB

One time you said your mother
liked me better than you
because you never asked her for recipes
but I did. Of course it wasn't true,
the part about who she liked best,
and yet, now that your mother is gone,
perhaps she would be pleased to know
I still have the recipes she wrote down
carefully on file cards, her cursive aligned,
each recipe neatly signed,
From the kitchen of Mrs. B.,
and that sometimes I still bake
her walnut and date bars,
the raspberry Matrimonials,
her famous Chocolate Crinkles.

Digging to China

Once I dug to China.
It was hard.
I had only a bent spoon
with a flowered handle.
The earth, like a broken pot,
was made of clay,
and all around me the bunch grass
stood tough and spiky,
its roots like box string
binding the earth together.

The first object I uncovered
was a rusty nail
from the fallen wooden gate
of a long-gone emperor.
Then a vole's tiny jawbone
like the shard of a broken teacup
came white to the surface.
I anticipated jars of oils and spices
and toys, made in the Far East
and lost by Chinese children.

If I suddenly broke through
to a child digging
from the opposite direction,
I would give her my hand
and pull her up into our yard.

All day long I labored
in the cause of international relations
till mother called me to dinner
and wouldn't take no for an answer.

The Photo Booth

I see your faces waiting for the train—
Chicago station. You were five and under,
all three of you, and thus your tickets free
though it cost more than money—loss of sleep,
the worry of two hands for three young children.

The ride across the country wasn't bad
though one of you threw up. The baby's
nosebleed finished off my last clean blouse,
and aged porters and waiters glared to see
us coming to the dining car. You spilled
your chocolate milk through several tablecloths—
mishaps regular as the train itself was not,
taking an extra night in Cheyenne where we
traipsed through that western city in vague search
of toys to eke out patience. I was crazy
to undertake a trip like that alone
but not alone of course with three young kids.

It was a year I always will remember,
the world in chaos, 1969.
I somehow thought that I could keep you safe
by taking that slow train back home. And look
how happy we all are in these four shots
inside the photo booth that afternoon.

You can't see the crumpled woman with DTs
on the soiled bench in that aging marbled station,
restored by now I'm sure—the place I mean,
the woman would have slipped away by now;
nor do we see the hoodlums at the door,
nor hear the traffic on the street outside
that screeched and roared. Two hands for three again
kept me inside to wait. The picture cannot
show remembered smells, the bathroom stalls
reeking of years of pee and cigarettes,
hot dogs steaming in their greasy bath,
the smell of sweating people in that room.

Instead it shows my face relaxed and calm.
I was so young, my hair so black back then,
and all of you, my puppy pack, each rising
to this occasion, making your funny faces.
I think we got four for a dollar in that booth,
or maybe less than that. So cheap a celebration
of what we did that summer. Though wars
went on and evil things occurred—the world,
as usual, a pinball game without restraint—
we all survived. How I loved, still love, your faces,
your spirits buoyant in any circumstance.

What about Those Ancestors?

Dear
Ancestors,
Thank
you
for
surviving.
Sincerely,
Your
Grate-
ful
Descend-
ant

What if you could fish for your ancestors in heaven,
casting far into the night sky when you can't sleep,
snagging Great-Great-Grandma and reeling her in
to tell you stories till 6 a.m.?

What if your ancestors are still watching you
and see everything you do? *Everything.*
Would you get sassy and say, *You did it too*?
Or just say—*Yes ma'am, No ma'am, Yes sir, No sir.*

What if they never really died but just piled up
in the back seat of your car, telling you how to drive,
telling you where to drive, drinking Scotch
from a silver flask and demanding ice cream.

What if you had no ancestors, just appeared
like a lonely bubble in a pool of tar? Pop!
Maybe your ancestors were jellyfish or one-celled
creatures without hairdos or mouths or underwear.

Whoever they were, invite them for a séance, a barbecue,
a tête-à-tête or a chin-to-chin, and if they come, celebrate
the nose you all share, your laugh, the color of your hair.
You might be an ancestor some day, maybe already are.

Something My Father Taught Me

Dodging and burning were skills
learned in the dark by practice.
Now no longer done delicately
with a wire and cardboard, a hole in paper,
or other handmade tool,
today's dodge and burn are digital,
but back when I watched
father in the darkroom
he showed me how to paint with light,
the image invisible till it went
into the developer. After developer
came the stop bath, then fixer, also called hypo.
After the picture was fixed you'd know
if you had dodged and burned right.
It took practice and you couldn't really tell
if you'd got it till later,
after the developing, the stopping, the fixing.
How I loved the quiet darkroom, the magic
of dodging and burning,
burning and dodging.

Greetings, A Photograph from Home

You can tell it's Christmas
by the spidery star hanging over Central
in a web of wiring
and by the string of lights in curlicues
outside the Chandler Coffee Shop.

On the wall of the building, a sign invites you
to the Skyroom Restaurant and Bar.
Streetlamp penumbrae make shapes
like flying saucers in the dark.

The street lined with big cars
shines in glossy black and white
and it's Coos Bay, circa 1959.
I know an ocean is at the far end of that street.
I would walk into this picture if I could.

Dreams of Possibility

Sometimes there is a closet full of fur coats
and sleeping at the back our old cat Cissy, who died.
I pet the cat—she purrs as I reach through the furs
to find a door which leads to narrow stairs.
Sometimes at the top of the stairway
there is a ballroom, no furniture,
but heavy velvet drapes frame windows.
The room smells musty but sweet.
I like the space, but when a figure glides out of the draperies,
face shrouded, hands shooting sparks
and smelling like fireworks, I am frightened and leave.
Sometimes there is a third floor.
I find it by a wooden fire escape on the outside wall.
The stairs are old. This could be dangerous
and yet I'm so happy to find new space
I can hardly contain myself. It's fun—
so many extra rooms and beds for everyone.

Six-on-Six

At thirteen I was tall
and could handle a basketball.
We played girls' rules, half-court—
Six-on-six they called it.
Every game I gave it my all,
dribbled twice, passed, ran, blocked,
got the ball back, pushed it hard
and high, into the basket. Yes!

After the last game of the season
I walked with Bob and Robert
to George's Market for ice cream.
You were high-point girl, they said
with obvious admiration.

Next year, at fourteen,
half a court was not enough.
I chose art club and school newspaper.
My basketball career was over.
And yet I remember with satisfaction
the year I was high-point girl.

The Piercing

Today I choose pearls
and remember my friend Etta
who pierced my ears
with an ice cube for an anesthetic
and a sewing needle for an instrument.
We weren't girls.
I was thirty and Etta only slightly younger.
A stay-at-home mother,
I had a hunger for experience
and some larger world, was restless
practicing my life without an audience.

Why putting holes in my ears
would make a difference
is not entirely clear but there were other things
I did as well that year.
I won't tell about them here.
I'll just say I liked the shiny rings
she slid into my bloody lobes, and that
I wore them sparkling on the train
when I took the children and
fled west that summer. 1969.

So long ago, yet consequence
continues, while random flights—
that is, of memory—
still entertain.

Her Regret

Dry eyes, dry eyes.
If only she had known
she would have saved
some of her young-woman tears
in long past years
for these old dry eyes
now that she no longer cries.

Class of Forever

Does anything ever seem more ordinary
than the way each day passes?
Cream-tipped clouds whistle by
faster even than in the movies.
Moments braided by desire
blend like colorful wires
of an electric circuit.
Old gentlemen in black coats
stand about inspecting the departing world,
wrinkles stamped by time
on their innocently licentious foreheads.
Young men and women carry their bodies
like brightly colored helium balloons
about to escape.

What do you remember? Is it
the shape of water stains on a white ceiling,
the white-on-white patterns in old wallpaper,
the feeling of a gravel road on bare feet?
The future comes to you through a plastic straw—

it almost quenches your thirst
and yet you can never get enough of it.
The past rolls up behind you like a carpet
being removed for cleaning, and yet,
there it is, at your heels, following you
like the stray dog you weren't allowed to keep.

Take up the billowing fabric
of days you didn't know wouldn't last,
bundle yourself as if
you were a saint ascending to heaven,
smooth your hair, and look good for the final picture
which will show you graduating
in the class of forever.

The Golden Light in Dreams

Last night I dreamed of a golden light,
round and bright as a Christmas orange.

A voice said: *You lived there once,*
and everything since is just a dream.

I took some comfort then,
that the bright light still burned.

One might live forever
caught in that glowing orb.

A long time has passed
since I curled in golden light

and yet last night it was still with me,
luminous in dreams.

2

Pilgrimage

Malheur, Steens, Alvord Desert

In May we go to the desert
to clean the ashes from our hearts.
The roughness of desert air is palatable,
like cracked wheat or burnt sugar.
There is grit in the wind,
and the sound of snipe winnowing in the grass.
We open ourselves to clear sky
and scour darkness from our thoughts.

We inhale and exhale slowly.
The mule deer march by in elegant processional.
Their radar ears turn this way and that.
Above the lake, white pelicans spiral up and down,
a double helix, a ballet about life and death.

The spring flowers of the desert glow with insane colors—
bright yellow buckwheat, blue penstemon, orange paintbrush.
Ascending the red slopes of Diamond Craters,
we stare into the great maar
which has been holding its basin of blue water
for six thousand years, as if waiting
for God to come down and drink here.

Wanting clean curves and distances, abstract shapes and long views,
for a while we leave behind what is too generous, too easy.
We go to the desert so we can return home to blurred edges,
and live again among forests, pastures, soft grasses.

Road Trip, Malheur

1

The two women working in the Fields café
both call their husbands *Dad.*
Dad and Dad come in to eat suppertime spaghetti,
as we do, hungry after our long drive across the state
from the Yamhill Valley. We've brought our homemade
westside wine to drink with dinner and offer a glass,
but one Dad tells us his choice is Franzia.
He drinks a tumbler of it with his spaghetti.

2

On the wall, a sign announces:
We have sold 829 famous milkshakes since Jan. 1.
We have sold 1056 hamburgers since Jan. 1.
It's only May. Before we leave this place we'll try both
and raise the bar a little. The BLM guy tells us,
this time each year milkshakes begin
to overtake hamburgers. By midsummer
milkshakes will rule.

3

The price for a motel room is displayed
on the back of the menu. Tempting—
last night we slept in the back of the truck
but today consider renting a room
because a storm is blowing in, wet and wind
that drove us off the back roads

we've been exploring. No good
getting stuck in desert gumbo,
but the few rooms have all been rented.
The truck will do. We have a mattress in the back,
warm sleeping bags, pillows, wool socks,
a watertight roof—sleeping spoon-fashion,
we don't need more than this.

4

Fields is home to half a dozen families and at least
that many dogs, most of which are lounging
in front of the store when morning comes.
Missing my dogs left at home,
I say howdy to these, scratch hairy chins.

5

Birds sighted this trip: bristle-thighed curlew (1),
black-crowned night herons (8), great
horned owls (2) with babies (2). The owlets,
not yet fledged, stare at us in the shade of black cottonwoods.
And there are yellow-headed blackbirds, avocets, willets,
whimbrels, red-legged stilts, killdeer, coots, cinnamon teal,
shovelers, tundra swans, sandhill cranes,
white pelicans, Canada geese, all more than we can count.
White-faced ibis like figures on the wall of an Egyptian tomb
flash purple and green iridescence in black.
One golden eagle on a telephone pole dries his feathers.

6

Our catalog of plants spotted includes
yampah, bitterroot, winterfat, wild onion, *Calochortus*,
paintbrush, lupine (*Lupinus biddlei* and others less rare),
larkspur, sagebrush, saltbush, phlox, *Ephedra* or Mormon tea. . . .
At the winterfat site, we climb a ridge and find
the bitterroot in bloom. Taste some, also wild onions,
yampa roots—all once harvested by American Indians here.
Yampa tastes a little like celery root or turnip. Bitterroot is astringent.
Noxious plants we see this trip include: cheatgrass,
knapweed, star thistle, peppergrass, Mediterranean sage.
Invasive species, like us, but we do our best to treat this landscape well.
We won't take root and spread
however much this place charms us.

7

Thirty-one miles north of Fields, Mickey Hot Springs
has been fenced from cattle since we were here last.
Under a chilly sky I soak my feet in the one tolerable pool—
my skin prickles, legs look greenish-white beneath water.
In other hot pots, mud boils and bubbles,
water would scald. The geyser is a foot-high spout.
Some of the pools are empty now, where water found its way
elsewhere, but you never know. On this fragile surface
we hear it boiling underground. It could come back.

8

On the playa in the Alvord Desert, a salt-white 12 x 5-mile area,
someone once set a land speed record, but racing
is now forbidden. We drive slowly to the middle, pose in the flatness
to have our pictures taken. *We were here.*

9

Next day the Dads are back for breakfast.
The storm has passed
and the kind ladies of Fields
have pancakes and bacon on the griddle.
Well fed, we will invest the day
in wildflowers, birds, distances, light.
Once I thought true Oregon
was only on the west side of the Cascades,
that east was wasteland.
Now I can't get enough of this broad sky.
this world we have ridden to its end
and its beginning.

The Killdeer's Ploy

Roadside, Harney County

I am weak, my legs are thin,
see how fragile I am?

I have a broken wing
I drag behind me, can't sing

but only make plaintive cry
to show how pathetically frail am I.

Come this way, follow fast,
Imagine I will be your sweet repast.

Ignore those gravel-colored eggs on bare and rocky ground.
Nothing there—nothing, nothing to be found.

The Art of Landscape

How the mountains echo yet vary one another's form,
near then far then farther in fading values.
How the clouds imitate the mountains' inclinations.
How trees define upright and landforms define horizontal.
How bushes and houses manage filling in
and the clouds define distance,
properly small on the bottom and larger on top
and yet vertical upon the canvas.
How the outlines of near objects are sharp
while distant lines are diffuse and of varying pressure,
and how human beings are tiny spots of color,
a means of fulfilling a longing
to find ourselves in the big picture.

Life Map: South Coast, Summer Place

I was thirty-five when I put money down
and paid ninety dollars a month
for a hillside of old fir, cedar, spruce,
thick forest duff underfoot, 700 feet of creek,
a trail leading to pasture. Here and there,
a giant stump with the axe-man's mark
where loggers stood six feet off the ground
to reach the saw point.
In some places, salal and fern adorned
a stump blackened from fire
that burned at least a hundred years ago.

Summers the family lived there wild,
bathed in the creek, boiled water
for dishes. Even in rain
we took long walks,
sat around the campfire.
One morning two peacocks
woke us with a sound like trains coming,
then flew away, never to be seen again.

Another dawn, I woke in the tent
with the rump of a large animal
pressing the canvas wall from outside.
It was Fred Anthony's donkey turned stray
eating the straw off our broom.
I read *Mother Earth News, The Whole Earth
Catalog, The Owner-Built Home*, built a shack
and dreamed of living off the land.
It never happened.
Another thirty-five years went by.

I go there when I can, and this year
finally got water and power. A little light,
a little heater in the shack, a better driveway.
Today, a frosty morning in November,
I had my first drink from the new well.
It was good cold water, not the fountain of youth,
but for a moment when I drank it I was still thirty-five.

Meditation, Sixes River

In the river
in my mind swimming
upstream it is always late summer there are

a few leaves
four or five or six that fall
gold they float downstream quickly neither spinning nor sinking

slowly deep breathing
and in my mind I am swimming upstream.
where a kingfisher calls and an ouzel walks underwater on stones

stone-eyed a weasel
watches from green rock in my mind
serpentine where reeds and ferns lean in from stony banks

in my mind
I do my slow breaststroke breathing
sliding through sweet cold water breathing deeply deeply breathing

Blanco: An Invitation

Come walk with me from Cape Blanco to the mouth of the Sixes,
a river of black sand and gold that long-ago miners followed for fortunes,
never richly granted but doled out in miniscule flakes of shining metal.

Have you heard the story about the man who lived upriver with two wives
mining the source of gold in the Sixes? He was suspicious
of anyone hiking that far who might abscond with his gold, or his wives.
The wives wore faded dresses made from old flour sacks,
and their plump bodies were covered with brown hair.
Apocryphal? Maybe not, this south coast never being quite settled.
Too poor and far from cities, too little populated,
steeped in Quiviran mythologies and Jeffersonian attitudes.
It is generally recommended, in these parts, that one stay clear
of a man with two furred wives and a gold claim on the Sixes.

Last night there was a full moon.
Today on the slopes of Blanco purple asters signal the end of summer—
sand-colored grass, cow parsley gone to seed, an uncommonly warm wind.
Below the Fresnel eye of the lighthouse, the beach is welcoming, expansive.
Minus tide, like an obsequious waiter, bows out before us,
leaving sand laid with delicate arrangements of shells, seaweed,
and silvered driftwood flushed downstream by the Sixes.
Along this beach, seals, sometimes an otter, follow our movements.
Upright in the water, dark-eyed, curious, the creatures look almost human.

On this apparently uninhabited stretch of sand
we find cunning houses built of driftwood,
each a perfect, inviting shelter but empty as if created by spirits
who live, like the Irish Sidhe, invisible in wind and fog.
They tempt one to stay and not go back across the mountains,
but those who never left are buried here in the old Irish graveyard.

There is a chapel in the vacated house
of the Catholic family who once lived here.
They logged and ran livestock in the marshy valley.
You might call it a spiritual place, or place of spirits.
On this very beach Bigfoot tracks appeared one year,
and a man dredging the river met Bigfoot numerous times,
a large figure minding its own business. Others said
orange glowing eyes were seen, uncanny noises were heard,
trees were ripped from their roots and twisted like braids of schoolgirls.
We use the passive, not to claim too much.
Some say a mermaid lives in the river, but I have never seen her myself,
so I have my doubts.

A few miles south is Battle Rock
where once an early expedition camped with a cannon.
Native people, possibly hostile, came to meet them. The white men fired.
Then retaliation. Many were killed on both sides.
Survivors told of a white man in a red shirt—
no one knew who he was. He came with the Indians.
Yet when the fight ended, as they left, the Natives kicked the body
of the man in the red shirt as it floated near shore.
The settlers changed their plans and went north.
Sometimes among the scant and wind-bent trees on Battle Rock
people see a glimpse of red homespun, but climbing the steep path
they find nothing.

I've got more stories. Tomorrow, let's walk
the south side of Blanco to the Elk River,
and hike the trail through the bogs at Blacklock.
Or if you prefer, we'll hike up Humbug Mountain.
It's steep but rewarding. Some soldiers once got lost there.
That's why they called it Humbug.

Aubade: Last Day in Camp

From an anxious dream of scarcity—
ragged fabrics, water and food meager,
blue and yellow lights
wavering on oily water—
I wake to the gobbling of wild turkeys
in the woods above the cabin.

I roll over to greet you
to find only the pillow, still showing
the press of your head, sheets warm
but you already up and gone.
Mourning doves in trees by the creek
tell me, go back to sleep,
but where is the joy
of sleeping in a solitary bed
with dreams so somber?

Outside—banging of a tailgate,
swish of zippers, thud of boxes.
Oh, cruel world that has
such efficiency in it.

I won't go.
I will lie here and stare at the cedar ceiling
till the pileated woodpecker
who comes at the end of August
sends his raucous call over the forest
and tells me it's time.

Blue River Night, September

We walked out in the dark to call for owls.
No owls answered
but the darkness and silence were sweet,

and we fell in love with the shadows
that surrounded us like big black bears
sniffing our hair, fondly petting our faces.

How to Wait

Be happy to stay in place.
From the window of your stalled train
watch leaves blown sideways, an eagle sliding
through air above the cottonwoods, rain.
Look at alder catkins in the trees beside the train track.
Wonder if that's the river you see,
shining silver beyond dike land,
or just another flooded field.

Study the dark flow of the slough
passing under a narrow bridge.
Try to see the invisible wind
that blew the tree onto the tracks.
Look for others that might fall. Look for the crew
coming back from clearing the rails.
Stare at the opposite tracks as you watch
for the freight train to come through, the one
that hit the fallen tree.

Sit up in your seat
as you hear the whistle of the freight coming north,

then see it—orange and black, rust-red,
car after car after car,
going to where you've just been. Breathe and sigh
as the freight train passes. Waiting was not so bad.

Now the train you're on begins to move again. And you
are leaving this place you looked at for two hours,
began to know just as it slipped away.
Peer into the distance. Let memory take you
back to every time you've come this way
and didn't even notice
that slough, that track, those alders,
that distant shining.

3

March Wind, Yamhill Valley

Just when we taste spring
and the million little frogs in the oak woods
have been peeping all night with joy,
here comes a windstorm with teeth like a wolverine.
It chews up the daffodils that are doing their best
to raise romantic poets from the dead.
It pulls at our doors like Bible-bearing proselytizers of a doomsday religion
or desperate salesmen insisting we buy air fresheners and toilet brushes.

Storms are so self-centered—they would rather be
exceptionally unhappy than ordinarily contented.
The storm throws itself against the windows, a bad drunk wanting in.
Its bitter tears of pathos and self-pity run down the double-paned glass.
The storm invokes familiar past storms—
its cousin who took down the oak tree and flattened three cars,
its uncle who collapsed our old barn one spring night,
leaving the sheep alive but *baaing* under splintered boards
so we had to pull them out, the sheep smiling and quickly forgetting
their near-death experience upon returning to the sodden pasture.

Today's storm declares itself to be our long-lost love child
and claims to need us though it really wants to pick our pockets,

empty our wallets and throw them into the bushes.
It has come from far away in a swooping pattern
like Chinese calligraphy meaning *chaos*. It has flown
over the Coast Range ridges and swept across the plant nurseries
where baby rose bushes shudder in dwellings of fragile plastic.
It has battered the vineyards and the old Flying-M ranch,
tormented the returning turkey vultures
and thrown the gliding marsh hawks off balance.
It has tossed the iridescent rock doves in the wheat field
and torn the vole from the mouth of the kestrel on the telephone wire.

It is a bully storm, a loud storm,
but I believe we will stare it down, and we can hope
it will clear the air for spring, which is coming.

Sunlight on Grass

Bill mows paths in the sheep pasture,
a maze to follow.
Playing hide-and-seek,
each grandchild runs a different direction.

Who can say no
to getting lost in high grass?
Each golden stem, each
narrow leaf and seed head
a conduit for light.
Today we are favorites
of the sun.

When I can't find them,
uneasiness creeps in.
Remembering Persephone,
I call out, *Olly olly oxen free.*
But they torture me by hiding longer.
Don't the old words work anymore?

Where are those children?
A swatch of blue cloth here,
a ribbon there, a telling flag of sunlit hair.
Aha, you are discovered.
Run, rabbits, run.

Grass seeds cover
the littlest grandson's head
like sesame seeds on a round bun.
Pasture wildflowers—

brodiaea, dandelions, daisies,
purple vetch, blue flax—
blend with reedy grasses
into woven bracelets
on child arms,
into crowns for hair.
Let's live here forever
in houses of green and golden grass.

Chase me, says a granddaughter,
six years old.
I do, but her young legs
are too fast for me.
Okay, I'll chase you, she offers,
and gives me a head start.
She counts to fifteen,
still not enough time.
Over and over I am caught.

July

prune faded roses
don't hold on to old flowers
second blooms are best

hot fields surrender
hay bales in tidy bundles
crows search for gleanings

dusty blue chicory
blooms on late summer roadsides
green sweat bees appear

Amazing Mavis

For a granddaughter

When the moon lights up like a red balloon
and the dog starts howling a dancing tune
and someone flies in on the back of a loon—
you can guess who it is, it's Mavis.

When the wind blows through like a fidgety bat
and the sky turns green and your tires go flat,
and someone appears in a purple hat,
wouldn't you know, it's Mavis.

She's not so big, she's just so tall,
but she's definitely there and she's not that small.
When you cook spaghetti she eats it all.
I think you know she's Mavis.

When cats wear shoes and cows wear pants
and the fleas in your socks begin to dance
and someone's required to take a chance,
it's time to call on Mavis.

There's no one anywhere quite so quite,
so much of a day and all of a night,
so very on top and so very much right,
so let's give a cheer for Mavis.

I have to admit this poem is so silly
it makes me sneeze like a dog eating chili.
Perhaps I should move to the outer Antilles,
but I want to stay here, near Mavis.

Combing a Granddaughter's Hair

Delphi's hair is a volcanic eruption,
a costume for rites of spring, a petaled blossom.
It is a dark fog, spume of sea water,
a sweet-scented mess of flowers.
When I comb Delphi's hair
I think of blue blossoms, dolphins,
a place of temples, mountains, a kind of hat.
It is a map of contrariness,
sweet smoke from an October bonfire.
Her hair makes ripples in the life stream,
draws myriad lines of ancestry.
Some days it's a soft cloud bringing gentle weather
and a net for catching rainbows. Yet it is also
her personal flag of independence.

Like a tangle of threads
in a sewing box, it can be sorted out
only with mindful concentration.

Wisdom

The road ahead like tarnished silver.
Rain in my hair, on my face—
good for the complexion they say,
prevents aging.
The crow in the walnut tree
laughs and laughs.

Wild Farm

First is the *Oemleria,*
also known as Indian plum,
and then the sandhill plums
pink and white.

Here come the *Erythronium,* aka
yellow dogtooth violet or fawn lily,
and the pink trout lilies.
Now the chocolate lily blooms
yellow and brown,
and in low wet places
the camas, a deep purplish blue.
Wild iris appear in the woods,
yellow violets, and the shooting stars.

Wild roses perfume the air
even before they bloom,
the deep pink Nootka rose, the rose
that is almost white, the pink
with a white eye, all wild roses.
And now the flax
shows up pale blue in the grass.
The orange columbine and the blue lupine
bloom on the bank at the bottom of the place
dangerously mingled with poison oak pollinating.

As each one goes
another comes on, the vetch and the clover,
the creamy white death camas
and the pink checker mallows
at the edge of the oak woods,

the blue-eyed grass
in the seeps of the vineyard,
the tiny white orchids in the shade
at the top of the pasture.

Now the elegant brodiaea,
a cone of blue in the ochre grass,
and the fool's onion, another brodiaea,
and the pink Hooker's onion
and onions with dark red corms
at the top. There are the late
obscure pink flowers, waxy and small,
which I don't know the name of.
The mule's ears bloom
in the hottest places.
The tiny yellow monkey flowers
smell like grass, and the lomatium
swallowtail larva feed on
decorates the south-facing slope
of the sheep pasture.

Now the grasses themselves,
past bloom, drop their seeds.
Now the flower of the Queen Anne's lace
floats above the pasture, and chicory,
blue as gaslight or a blind eye,
blooms along the roadside.

Soon it will all be finished again.
The plums will fall, the berries will dry,
the sharp and clinging seeds disperse
and the mushrooms sprout
their fruits in the autumn rain.
What does it all mean?
It is just an old story
the farm tells over and over.

Born

Out in the barn at 4 a.m.
I found a new lamb, wet, black, staggering
under the weight of being born.
As I toweled it off, the mother raised a fuss
so I turned out the light, called the dogs,
went back to bed and dreaming.

Sometimes when the puppy yelps I dream
of getting up and letting her out at 4 a.m.
or 5:00, then wake and remember the dogs
haven't been out yet. I rise, staggering
through the dark house, trying not to make a fuss
or wake Bill. Each day is like being born

again, they say. We don't remember being born,
gulping air, howling that first howl, except perhaps in dreams,
and I imagine it's a good thing we don't. What a fuss
it must have been, the water, the blood at 4 a.m.,
the loss of warmth and safety, staggering
to meet the cold new world. I hear the dogs

now at the door. They're good dogs,
border collies, smart and quick. Born
with the instinct to work. It is staggering
to realize how much they know already. Dogs dream.
We know it by the sounds they make at 4 a.m.
or in the daytime when they sleep, running, making a fuss.

It's funny to see them fantasize in sleep like that, to fuss
over chasing a cat that isn't there. Our dogs
sleep by the bed so when they dream I know what hour a.m.
it is. My mother told me I was born
at 9:00 in the morning. At 6:00 or 7:00 I'd still like to dream
but I get up, staggering

to the kitchen for coffee. I look out at the staggered
trees in the orchard, the deer passing through. Breakfast is no fuss,
just coffee, maybe muffins, the newspaper. I dream
of going back to bed but instead go out with the dogs
who love waking, and we find another lamb, like magic, born
after the other. Who knows what hour a.m.?

Walking around the Place: November

The dogs charge ahead as we walk
but we are leisurely, look for
each sign of scat, each mushroom.
We mark how yesterday's wind
took down the last yellow leaves in the vineyard
and something has been eating and shitting pears.
Something has been digging for truffles or grubs.
Something has clawed the bark from a leaning oak branch.
At the base of these trees are shredded fir cones.

From the highest place, we look at neighboring wheat fields,
vineyards, and horse pastures. To see if it is still standing,
we check the northern fence where cows next door lean over.
We study the muddy trails of creatures going to and fro—
skunks maybe, or coyotes or barn cats or deer.
We comment on how blackberries, recently trimmed back,
already lean in along the pathways,
snagging our jackets with their brambles.
We pause at the sinking indentation of the old sheep's grave
and the vacancy where the striped coralroot bloomed in April.
We admire the moss garden on the rotten plank,
and the lichens and lungworts in the forest.
At the bottom of the pasture, we approve
the winter pond slowly filling with rainwater,
the yellow crab apples still hanging,
though the leaves are gone.

The Tale of Toffee

Toffee was an old sheep, ten years at least,
with soft gray wool and a monkey-like
dark face, five years old when we got her.
For all we knew she'd never had a lamb.
Each fall the ram showed interest but
when spring came, no lamb for Toffee.
The other ewes had lambs each year.
One at a time, as they lambed,
they got special treatment.
Into the lambing pen they went, each
with her own pan of COB—
corn, oats, barley—and molasses,
some alfalfa, her own water dish,
and after the great ordeal
a sliced apple for refreshment.

They got to stay there in their own apartments
with their lambs for a day or so
and didn't have to push and shove
at the feed box, just spent the first day
licking their lambs and nickering to them,
nibbling COB and sipping cool water.
Toffee never had that chance and now it looked
as if she never would. She was rather fat
and liked her supper, and it's true
at feed time Toffee knew how to throw her weight
around to get the best place for alfalfa
and other treats.
There was nothing demure about Toffee—

she was a regular battle-axe at the food trough.
But sometimes, through February and March,
we saw her staring at the new lambs
and their mothers, the other ewes.
Then it seemed the gray curls around her large
dark monkey-face would tremble somewhat,
though maybe we imagined it.
I should admit that Toffee was sometimes
the object of undeserved laughter. For example,
the time she rolled over and couldn't get up.
When she didn't arrive for dinner after dark,
we went out with the dogs and flashlights,
searched far and wide, finally found Toffee
on her back and helpless, her legs sticking up.

We rolled her over and she stood, trotted
to the lit barn anticipating dinner
with little or no appearance of distress.
So that was Toffee, Miss Toffee we called her, fat
sheep with a girlish yet elderly look.
(It was the gray curls.)
This spring she seemed a little lethargic
and we worried she was in decline.
Then one day she went to the upper woods
and stayed all day in the oaks,
not eating grass or anything, just
looking fixedly over the downhill pasture
where the other ewes grazed and nickered
to their lambs. All morning she stayed there.

She looked moody and didn't even lie down
till about noon. Then, no fuss, she had a ewe lamb.
She nickered and licked it and stood between it
and us when we came around to look at it.
It had floppy ears and was coal black.
It staggered around and found the teat,
nursed and fell asleep in the grass.
When evening came we led her into the barn
with her new lamb, opened the door of the
lambing pen. She moved in as if she owned it.
We gave her an apple for a treat
and grain with molasses, her own
water dish and alfalfa. She nickered
at her lamb and nibbled COB.

She sipped her water noisily as sheep do,
like drinking through a straw. Licked her lamb
some more and lay down with it. It was
clearly apparent she really liked it.
The other sheep put their heads between the rails
and tried to get Toffee's special dish
but they couldn't reach it. They were discomfited
to see Toffee in there instead of themselves,
but Toffee was pleased to have a turn
to live in the lambing pen for a day,
to have her own lamb and her own apartment.
She sniffed the lamb's tail and nickered to it.
The lamb nickered back, staggered up, nuzzled,
then nursed at Toffee's teat, the udder bigger than it was.

A.M. Prometheus

When I hear the crinkle and crackle of newspaper,
the thumping and clanging, the bump and the banging,
the wallop, the whack and the smack, the thud of wood,
the rattle of metal, the click and snap of a match
as you start the morning fire,
I roll over; hide my face in my pillow
from red sunrise, gray fog, or cold rain streaming
and happily anticipate how I will soon stand
with my back to the fire, drinking coffee
and toasting my backside.
Husband, I hope you know I appreciate you,
and all this hullaballoo.

Working

So much instinct, so much intelligence,
in the energy of a black and white dog.
I wish I were better at this, my instinct
sharp as hers, my feet quick as hers.
I am trying to learn.

I go this way, the sheep go that way.
She circles and the sheep follow me.
She turns them by the direction their noses take
and we are a whirlpool of wool,
me stomping heavy in my boots,
Maggie light on her white paws.
Come by, away to me, walk up, that'll do . . .
I hope we are getting our signals straight.

Rasping crows fly over. Their cries
and the smell of rotting onions
from the field across the road
roughen the atmosphere,
a little rain falls, and cold
creeps into my knees.
But she is mine and I am hers,
and for a moment at least
the sheep belong to both of us.
With dogs, this game we play
is called working.

Sharing the Couch

Border collie Maggie has a nose like a fox, is black and white
and often sits on the best couch where she is not
supposed to be. She looks so happy it's hard to say, *Down, dog,*
as she stares at me with eyes that are coppery and bright
as wet river stones. When I move into her place it's comfortably hot
where she was sitting this chilly day, and I ask myself, *Why hog*
this all to myself? so I call her back.
Soon she is sleeping like a log with her head on my belly.
My own mind and body go pleasantly slack
petting the dog.

Today's News

At the other end of our road
the migrant workers' house by the big vineyard is empty again.
The dumpster in the driveway is overfull
and a Cap'n Crunch box lies crushed in the grass.
Two television sets are overturned on the gravel,
heavy old-style tubes, gray like blind eyes.
It's January. The grapevines,
pruned neatly back to sticks, promise nothing,
and yet I believe the kestrel on the telephone wire
is enjoying her morning mouse,
whose limp tail dangles like an untied shoestring.

Solstice

The orchid you gave me in winter now in June has begun to fade, its multiple blossoms turning from silk to wrinkled paper. Summer begins, yet once again each long day will grow shorter like a candle burning on a birthday cake. Nothing to cry over but I remember that my father marked the longest day with muted regret and a shot of whiskey, as he noted there would never be another day longer than this one, the year's hinge, a door's slight closing. So it goes with the orchid which I had begun to hope would bloom forever, so florid, freckled, increasing and incessant its multiple flowerings. Dear one, I remember it was cold and dark when you placed it on the sill of the window and there was snow outside, an unexpected storm that filled our country road with white and drifting powder. We warmed ourselves by admiring the grace of the red and white blossoms on our side of the double-paned window, a tropical illusion of heat and sunshine in a cold white world, a comfortable self-deception as the days steadily grew longer. Now, just as winter once fed out the spool of lengthening daylight, bright summer begins to wind in the hours. Thank you, my love, for the orchid, whose beauty has accompanied us thus far, and yet I must say how much I resist this fading, the way the world like a flower shows us so much heat, so much light, so much beauty even as it shortens the leash.

Getting to Know You

Is your heart a fortress?
I cautiously wave the white flag of my interest.

Is your heart a first-aid station?
I will bring you the skinned knees of my life.

Is your heart a tool chest?
So much needs fixing.

Suddenly behind a swinging door
I hear music and laughter.

Olé! Your heart is a cantina.
There will be singing and dancing.

Poranges

An orange leaf was laid on every finger bowl
in the ancient kingdom of citrus.
Orange is the cousin of gold
with none of its symbolic worth
but more alive.
Orange is sometimes angry
but only singes, never burns.
Orange is the missing flavor
in the gelatin salad at the church potluck.
An orange will bring you vials of sunshine
to carry you through the winter.

Once I was the orange
in a dream of California in 1941.
I am in love with every painting
named *Still Life with Oranges.*
Orange is the famous word without a rhyme,
a sound like no other
that makes you want to invent a new language
with words like *forange* and *courange*
in order to write a sonnet about oranges.

Who was William of Orange
and how did he get to be so superior?
In the Orangerie in Paris
we wandered hand in hand
like fantastical koi
swimming among the water lilies of Monet.
This morning's sunrise was the color of a blood orange,
but when I walked out to meet you on the road,
it had already started to rain.
In the pocket of my raincoat
there was an orange.

4

Intimations

The pot boiling over,
shingles torn off by the wind,
the hawk at the bird feeder,
the door loose on its hinge,

the sound of distant sirens,
a knife misplaced, it was here a moment ago,
a helicopter thrumming over trees,
a scrabbling sound outside the window.

I sit with my coffee
and confront the morning newspaper.

January Night

No rain, but the sky
is black like fur on a wet dog.
Though it's 4 a.m. and dark out
I hear the rooster crow.
He hears me in the house
and wants to announce he's still on the job.

We are all doing our best, rooster.
Go back to sleep with your eight hens,
you fortunate fellow.
Only owls, poets, and crazy birds
are up at this hour.

Farm Years

One brown, one blue eye, handsome Jack
is under the bedroom window
guarding us all night long.
Maggie is just beyond, near the pink rose bush,
dreaming of flocks of sheep.
Shy Molly is under the lilacs,
her tender brown eyes asleep.
Black and white Guy
is between the quince trees.
That accounts for the dogs.
Valencia, the gray cat found in Tucson
on a street named Valencia,
is buried next to the Turkish fig.
Most of the cats were strays—
no wonder I keep forgetting
where they have all gone.

Fog Changes Things

On our walk this morning
through white February air it seemed
as if no one else was in this world
and nothing in it but white wisps
and dead crowns of Queen Anne's lace
crusted with frost.
Suddenly there appeared cattle
on the neighbor's farm, longhorns
like gentle Minotaurs peering at us.
Then they were gone and a horse came,
whinnying across white space,
a friendly Pegasus. Beyond and invisible,
a barn radio played music
like background for a movie,
the last scene when everything was over
and gain or loss or love or hate
settled at last. Of course
the horse soon floated off, and on a hill
out of the fog white wizard wands appeared,
thousands arranged as symmetrically as crosses
in Normandy, but these were protective wraps
on hazelnut trees planted in December.
Then once more we descended into swirling mist,
for mist swirls like water in a cauldron
and thoughts while walking. Again it was
as if we were nowhere, and maybe we were.

The Hot Walk

On one side the wheat is golden and ripe.
On the other, a vineyard
sprawls across the hillside
like a corpse in a Jacobean play.
The Queen Anne's lace
spreads its carroty smell
on the landscape,
and everywhere grass
is dry as needles.

At the corner
where the dusty road turns right,
bees aimlessly circle their white hives
as if wondering what happened
to dewy mornings,
the honey of spring clover.
We meant to take this walk for pleasure
and for betterment,
but the heat has turned it into
a kind of suffering,
a medieval exercise
in purification.

Even the dogs meander along
in a desultory manner.
They keep throwing themselves
into the shade of ditches.
I hope we can make it back.
I hope we have not come too far.

Lilac Hill Road

I celebrate my road which is a tongue tasting the world,
a ribbon tying the earth together like a gift,
the place I have landed. This road
whose name describes the magic of topography
and offers lavender bouquets of sweet-smelling flowers.
I sing of my road whose name bears numbers for counting and adding up
so that messages can arrive in a timely fashion,
whose name resonates of compass, winds, and the intricate labors
   of cartographers.
My road lends me its identity so that others can find me
and so I can venture out and find my way back
by this road which is mine and yet also shared with others.
My road kindly orders the dwellings along it for peace of mind.
It rises and falls in hills and hollows,
yet gives me a steady place in the universe,
so I can say I am a recognized, situated person.

Passage

Drunk on hawthorn berries
the waxwings assemble
on autumn branches.
All tweeting and chirping at once,
like my relatives
they interrupt one another's conversations
and also like my relatives
none among them takes offense.
Soon they will go elsewhere,
making their way south,
but for now they are happy
for the convivial atmosphere
and the good booze.

Autumn Fugue

The garden spills
its giant's share of wealth,
tomatoes in royal opulence,
squash like ancient fertility objects.

Now here comes the frost,
here come the darkening days.

The beans are overgrowing their pods—
like young men in tight jeans.
Gather potatoes while you can,
the large, the small, the ungainly.

For here comes the drenching rain,
the cold, the spirit-quelling.

Pull the onions quickly,
their many layered domes like frosted glass.
Shuck the seeded corn. Gather eggplants
that flop and dangle like purple breasts.

Here comes the hand
that closes the eyes of the corpse.

Let the last sowing of cilantro
sweeten its seeds, each one fragrant,
a world in itself. Gather the basil,
it will not survive much longer.

Oh, here come the darkening days,
the grave mound that sinks slowly.

The last wormy radish and the overblown broccoli
blossom, even as earth withdraws her sweetness,
pulling her veil over her face,
shutting her eyes against abundance.

Here come the days,
the darkening days.

Lie down in the dirt,
pull the last of its warmth into your belly.
Here are the darkening days.
All that is passes into memory.

Three in Late Winter

The low winter sun
casts light on our gravel road—
small Stonehenge shadows.

Crescent moon woman
sinks onto her back in dark
pillows—the Coast Range.

Geese call in the night.
I look up to see them pass
and find Jupiter.

n Memory of Molly, A Border Collie

And a nod to André Breton

My dog whose teeth were tiny forests of ivory,
whose tail was a dark storm out of the north,
whose eyes were flecks of wood fire
burning all night in the fireplace,
whose ears turned like antennae on a ship far out to sea,
whose toenails beat clicking rhythms across the linoleum floor,
whose toenails were cicadas, snail shells, the tapping of tiny pencils,
my dog whose fur rolled like the ocean
on a deserted beach—
my dog whose black lips sometimes smiled,
sometimes pursed into a howl—
my dog with the bark of a lion and a monkey combined,
my dog who howled like an arctic train engine warning
the polar bears off the tracks,
like a woman who has lost her favorite earring,
who howled as if calling us home from Jupiter,
my dog whose snore when she slept
was the warm hearth I came home to.

Moon Fever, 2017

Our moon that blocked the sun
and strutted for our awe not long ago
is feverish red tonight,
smoked by forest wildfires.

Unlike the sixty-seven
dancing moons of Jupiter
or the two gallstone moons of Mars,
unlike Saturn's Busby Berkeley show
or Venus and Mercury's moonlessness,
our singular moon in health
is silvery, elegant, cool.

What can we do
to cure this firestorm ague
but look and pray the fever breaks
and that our dear romantic moon,
our crescent, our shining plate,
our silver spoon,
regains her soothing pallor.
Dear moon, we're sorry.
Please recover soon.

Daily Business

Early summer again, this sunshine tastes like butter and lemon.
A yellow agate in the gravel beckons—I can't stop collecting stones.

On this morning's walk a sweet smell comes, seductive as Polynesian flowers.
Now I see it is wheat, each ripening stalk like a paint brush dipped in sunlight.

The lazuli bunting sings in the roadside hedge, hiding his turquoise melody.
My hands on his leash, the dog's rough energy pulls me through the morning.

Voices of workers in the vineyard are faint music,
their silhouettes against the skyline like shadow puppets.

All these rocks I've carried home over the years—
I should return them to the mountain before the mountain comes to get them.

Friday Night Aphrodite

Imagining myself a pearl, I lie
surrounded by iridescent bubbles—
the old claw-foot tub Bill salvaged
from behind the barn, my oyster shell.

Orange, lime blossom, scent of geranium,
patchouli, lavender, hay . . . a steamy garden.
The lotus on the label of my bubble bath
in ad-writer's chatter telegraphs cleanliness:
Found in murky waters, the lotus
produces blossoms radiant and pure.
I yawn: So *true.*

Dried hands hold this week's *New Yorker*
in steam above the waterline,
as I savor art, wit, the far-off urbane.
From time to time, a blind toe reaches,
adds hot water to cooling.
In a steamy glass, ice water sits
tub-side, convenient to sip.

Slowly I turn from pearl to roasted fowl,
pink and wrinkling, toenails clipped,
offensive stubble stripped, well done.
Time to rise, feeling both ancient and new,
from shimmering bubble blue light
cupped in this tub of white. Sweat, worries,
dirt, old skin, maybe even sin, wash down
the drain, a convolute metaphor.

Sing praise for Friday night ablutions,
and like a lotus in murky waters, rise
from this leisurely bath, purified
after a week of hasty showering.

Mileage

As I sit waiting for the tow truck,
I realize I've never before had a car so long.
Twelve years, 187,000 miles. Time to move on.

Come to think of it
I've never lived in one place as long
as I've lived where I live now, thirty years.

Of course I've never been this old before either.
Since there's nothing to do till the tow truck comes
I'll just sit here singing my short long song.

r, Ready-Made

My new car makes me think of Marcel Duchamp,
with its clean black seats and its buttons,
its turning ratio and electronic devices,
the warning beep if I am about to back into something,
Bluetooth & hands-free communication system,
six-month free trial subscription to Sirius
which I most likely will never renew but will miss when it's gone—
classical, rock, news, all without static—
little pockets for loose change, sunglasses, and other objects,
wheels that look like Modernist chrome daisies,
multiple cup holders and a key with remote buttons
to lock, unlock, open, close, to blow the horn and locate,
lights that turn themselves off if I forget to,
blind-spot mirrors and remote rotating side mirrors,
telescoping steering wheel adjustable to various positions,
heater, air conditioning, multiple air vents with swivel openings,
red, white, and blue lights on the dashboard
that tell me so many things I can't keep track of them all—
miles per gallon, miles till empty, miles for trip A and trip B, total miles.
Notice the quietness of it, the mild roar when I accelerate,
the windows that go up and down at a touch. I know
it is a modest car, a middle-class car, a midsize car.
It is a car an old lady can drive for the rest of her life. And yet
I imagine Marcel Duchamp might have painted this car
with all the windows going up and down at once,
doors opening and shutting, music playing, phone ringing,
backup warning signal beeping. He would have noticed the glitter
in the discreet gray paint. He would have liked how it traverses
a multiplicity of time zones—now here, now there, now here again.
He would have called the painting *Gray Car Descending Lilac Hill Road*.
Oh, ride with me in spirit, Marcel Duchamp, oh, ride in my new car.

Mystery

I like the look of things behind things,
a country church steeple behind a line of autumn maples,
ash trees in a swale beyond a white farmhouse,
the aspect changing as we move down the road.

I like the silhouette of a large house
slightly over a hill, the silhouette shifting
as we walk nearer and nearer until
the house sinks and you see only the hill.

I like to see a child peeking around a corner,
a cat staring out from under the edge of a newspaper,
a foot dangling out of bed from beneath a blanket,
the top of an uncombed head behind an open book.

In cities I like the tops of old buildings behind other buildings,
the tops with their renderings of ancient geometries,
their stories of years and fashions and seasons
more alluring than foundations and entrances,

I like dunes behind dunes and the sea beyond them,
mountains behind mountains in shades of gray, green, blue.
And the sky beyond that. Is there anything behind it?
If there were, I'd like that too.

Without Us

The scented flower
that blooms and blushes
unseen by human eyes
is by white-tail doe, honeybee,
and hungry mouse
recognized.

Schrödinger's cat's fleas
know where the cat is
and whether it's alive or dead
or whatever.

In the forest no tree
falls without a sound—
keen ears
of wood rats,
squirrels, bears,
and deer abound.

A Quartet in Time

Sun up—Trask Mountain
wears a white blanket of snow.
I let black hens out,
the valley still in shadow,
faint skunk smell—time for coffee.

Now snow snakes arrive,
winds slither across pavement,
white on black asphalt.
Oh, weather always changing,
more amusing than TV.

Our marmalade cat
spies me through falling snowflakes,
makes dainty paw prints,
purrs as he runs to greet me—
is it true love or cat treats?

I'm fed up with snow.
Today drippy half-formed flakes
do not excite me,
no longer my cold delight.
I pray for weather to change.

ut Time

expect the final moment of my life to last forever, just as the first one has.
I expect to meet my maker who will look like my grandfather smoking a
    cigar, my grandmother braiding her hair before bedtime, a newborn
    infant, or a native prairie in the American Midwest.
I expect a tremendous wind to sweep across the landscape and leave
    nothing standing but the blackberry thicket at the bottom of my
    property.
I expect time and tide will wait for a respectful moment and then rush on.
I expect in 150 years no one now walking on the earth will be alive and yet
    we will all still be here.
I expect a ladder made of blue silk ribbons will fall from the sky and I will
    slowly ascend to somewhere.
I expect my spirit to go on watching over all of you, being entertained and
    dismayed yet hopeful.
I expect time is an illusion created by memory.
I expect time to come to a stop when I die.
The earth will disappear and rain will not know where to fall.

Corner Office

Executive of my own retirement, I have a corner office
with windows facing north and west. Bonus adjacent kitchen.

Outside the road is sheeted with ice, no way to town.
The sky is the color of pencil marks badly erased on newsprint.

Brown hairs on the barbed-wire fence
show where hungry deer passed through last night.

The old abandoned pump house leans like a drunk,
supported by barren brambles of a wild rose bush.

As ice melts, fog rises, the pasture barely visible past the driveway.
The day dissolves like sugar in a glass of water.

Sometimes memory is like that.
Outside at the bird feeder, sparrows give way to scrub jays.

I remember mornings I rose, drove to work, came home tired at night.
Day by day the road, the job, the place—it all became familiar.

I straighten my desk, read mail, and look out the window,
make heartfelt resolutions for a new year. There is much to be done.

Acknowledgments

The author wishes to thank the editors of the publications in which the following appeared.

Cloudbank: "About Time," "Autumn Fugue" (previously in
You Rarely See Such Things Any More, Side Porch Press 2013),
"Friday Night Aphrodite."

These Mountains That Separate Us (Traprock Press, 2013):
"Road Trip, Malheur."

Raising Lilly Ledbetter: Women Poets Occupy the Workspace (Lost
Horse Press, 2015): "The Typist."

Windfall: A Journal of Poetry of Place: "Blanco: An Invitation"
(as "Walking Blanco"), "Kansas 1914-1992" (as "Kansas"),
"Life Map: South Coast, Summer Place" (as "Life Map: South
Coast"), "March Wind, Yamhill Valley," "Milky Coffee," "Pilgrimage,"
"Sunlight on Grass."

You Rarely See Such Things Any More (Side Porch Press, 2013):
"The Seventy-Five-Year-Old Woman Has Seen Wonders in Her Life,"
"The Piercing," "My First Butcher."

Epigraph page quotation from *The Confessions of St. Augustine*,
translated by J. G. Pilkington (New York: Heritage Press, 1963).

Appreciations

I offer my deep and sincere love and appreciation for the support I have had from so many amazing writer friends, including: poet, editor, and inspiration, Erik Muller; The Side Porch Poets, Ursula Le Guin, Molly Gloss, Noël Hanlon, Caroline Le Guin, Bette Husted, Kari Easton, and Jeannette Cappella, a lifeline over the years; Alice Derry and Clem Starck, wonderful poets and astute readers of poetry; and my first reader, companion in adventure, and dear husband, William Beckman. I especially want to thank friends and *Windfall* editors, Michael McDowell and Bill Siverly, whose aesthetic and editorial vision has provided a home for poetry to thrive, in particular, poetry of the beautiful Northwest.

About the Author

Barbara Robertson Drake was born in Kansas in 1939 and moved west via old Route 66 in 1941, riding between her parents on a small wooden box (for the view) on the seat of their new Chevrolet pickup, all their belongings in the back. The family eventually landed in Coos Bay, Oregon, where Drake grew up and graduated from Marshfield High School. She later attended the University of Oregon, receiving her BA in English in 1961. After spending a year exploring Europe by motor scooter with her husband, Albert Drake, and another year living in a stone cabin in the woods outside Portland and giving birth to their son, Moss, she returned to the University of Oregon as a TA and graduate student. Her daughter Monica was born during a spring finals week. Drake received her MFA in creative writing in 1966 and subsequently lived in Michigan for sixteen years, where her daughter Bellen was born. She taught at Michigan State University for several years before returning to Oregon to teach creative writing and literature at Linfield College from 1983 to 2007. She also served as a visiting writer at Whitman College in Walla Walla and at Lewis and Clark College in Portland. Now a Linfield College English Professor Emerita, she lives with her second husband, William Beckman, on a small Yamhill County farm in the foothills of the Oregon Coast Range, where they enjoy walks with their two border collies and introducing their grandchildren to country life.

Windfall Poetry Series

1. Bill Siverly, *The Turn: Poems and Reflections 1987-1997*
2. Barbara Drake, *Driving One Hundred*
3. Ingrid Gottschalk, *What Remains / Was Bleibt,* translated from the German by Jutta Donath and Daniella King
4. Michael McDowell, *The Hundred-Year House*
5. Bill Siverly, *Steptoe Butte*
6. Penelope Scambly Schott, *Lovesong for Dufur*
7. Bill Siverly, *Nightfall*
8. Barbara Drake, *The Road to Lilac Hill: Poems of Time, Place, and Memory*

Colophon

The titles are set in 14-point Cochin, a serif font with a low x-height and long ascenders designed in 1912 by the Parisian foundry Georges Peignot et Fils and named for Charles-Nicolas Cochin, an eighteenth-century engraver, designer, and art critic. In 1977 Cochin was adapted and expanded by Matthew Carter for Linotype.

Robert Slimbach designed the text font, Warnock, a variation on the original wedge-serifed font named after John Warnock, one of the founders of Adobe. The version used within this volume is 11-point Warnock Pro, which Adobe released as a commercial font in 2000.

This volume was digitally printed by the book manufacturer Thomson-Shore in Dexter, Michigan, on 60-pound Nature's Natural, an acid-free premium book paper made by Glatfelter and certified under Forest Stewardship Council standards.